EASY PIANO

# THE BEST OF THE EAGLES

### Arranged By

# DAN COATES

EXCLUSIVELY DISTRIBUTED BY

HAL•LEONARD®

Project Manager: Carol Cuellar

# Dan Coates

One of today's foremost personalities in the field of printed music, Dan Coates has been providing teachers and professional musicians with quality piano material since 1975. Equally adept in arranging for beginners or accomplished musicians, his Big Note, Easy Piano and Professional Touch arrangements have made a significant contribution to the industry.

Born in Syracuse, New York, Dan began to play piano at age four. By the time he was 15, he'd won a New York State competition for music composers. After high school graduation, he toured the United States, Canada and Europe as an arranger and pianist with the world-famous group "Up With People."

Dan settled in Miami, Florida, where he studied piano with Ivan Davis at the University of Miami while playing professionally throughout southern Florida. To date, his performance credits include appearances on "Murphy Brown," "My Sister Sam" and at the Opening Ceremonies of the 1984 Summer Olympics in Los Angeles. Dan has also accompanied such artists as Dusty Springfield and Charlotte Rae.

In 1982, Dan began his association with Warner Bros. Publications - an association which has produced more than 400 Dan Coates books and sheets. Throughout the year he conducts piano workshops nationwide, during which he demonstrates his popular arrangements.

# Contents

# THE BEST OF MY LOVE

Words and Music by
DON HENLEY,
GLEN FREY and JOHN DAVID SOUTHER
*Arranged by DAN COATES*

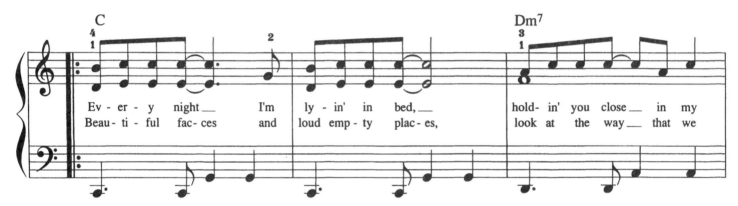

Ev - er - y night ___ I'm ly - in' in bed, ___ hold - in' you close ___ in my
Beau - ti - ful fac - es and loud emp - ty plac - es, look at the way ___ that we

dreams; think - in' a - bout ___ all the things that we said and
live; wast - in' our time ___ on cheap talk and wine

com - in' a - part ___ at the seams. We tried to talk it
left us so lit - tle to give. That same old crowd was like a

The Best of My Love - 4 - 2

6

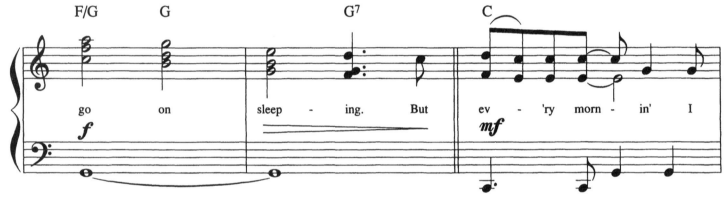

The Best of My Love - 4 - 3

way. You know we al-ways had each oth-er, ba - by,

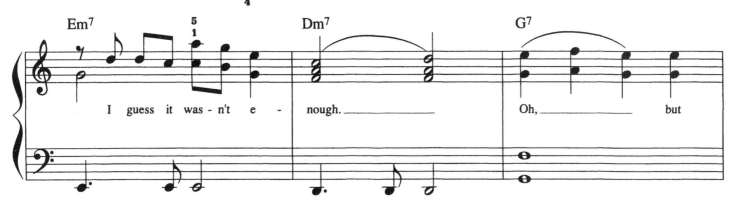

I guess it was-n't e - nough. _____ Oh, _____ but

here in my heart ___ I give you the best ___ of my love.

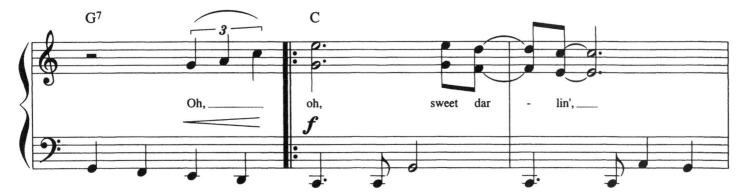

Oh, _____ oh, sweet dar - lin', ___

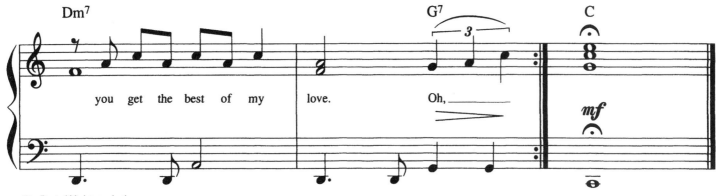

you get the best of my love. Oh, _____

# DESPERADO

Words and Music by
DON HENLEY and GLENN FREY
*Arranged by DAN COATES*

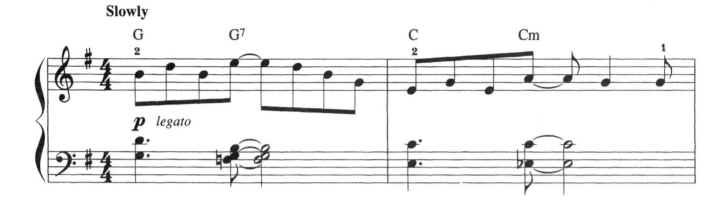

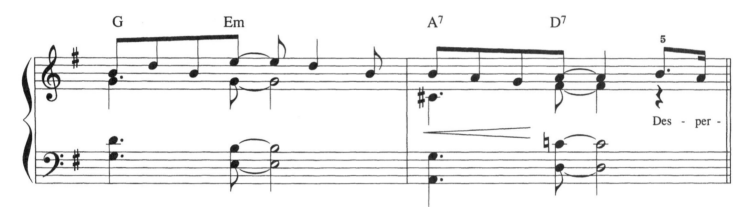

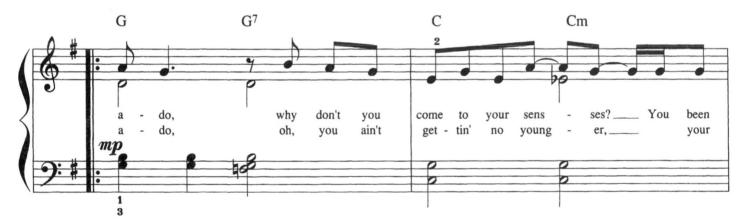

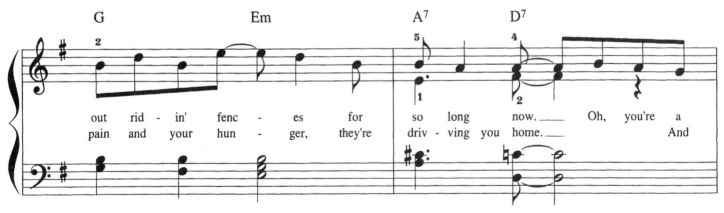

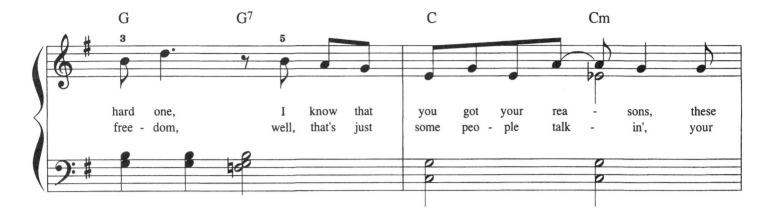

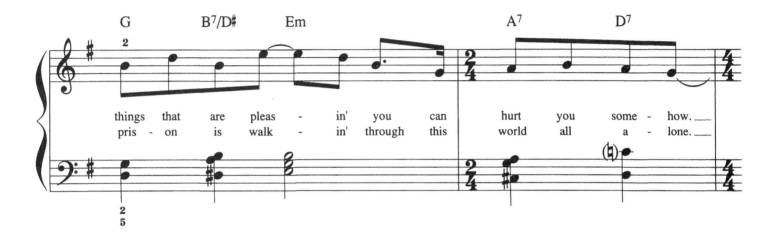

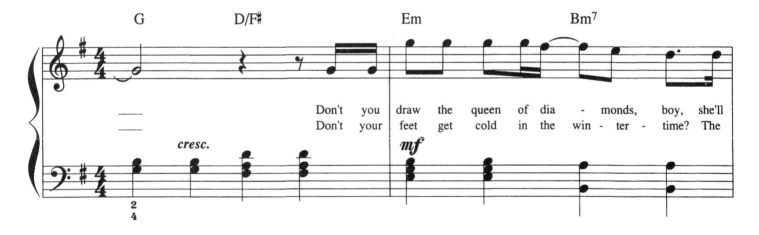

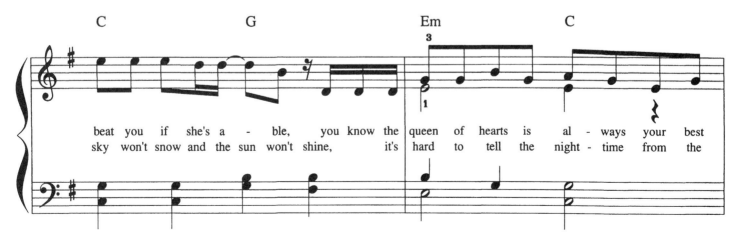

Desperado - 4 - 2

10

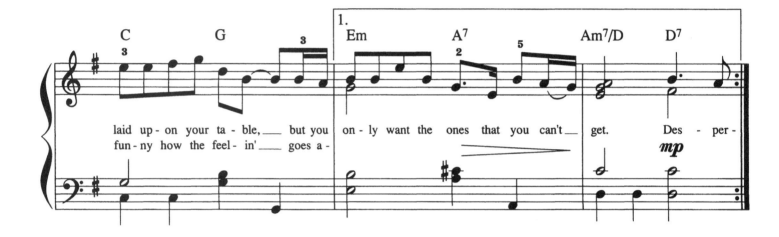

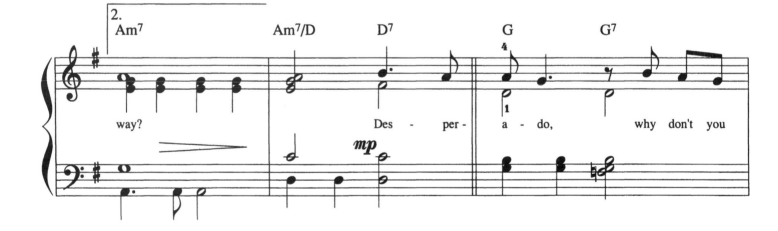

Desperado - 4 - 3

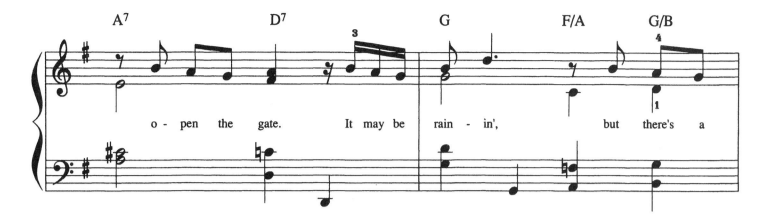

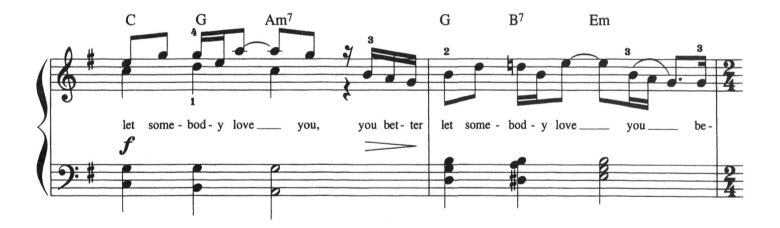

# HOTEL CALIFORNIA

Words and Music by
DON HENLEY, GLENN FREY and DON FELDER
*Arranged by DAN COATES*

**Moderate Rock beat** ♩ = 128

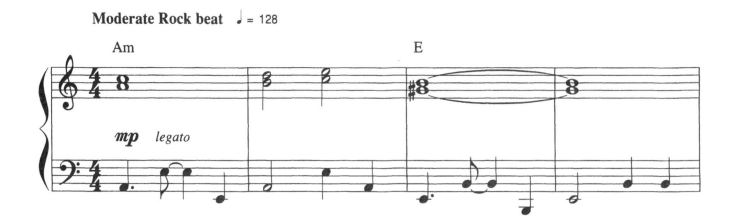

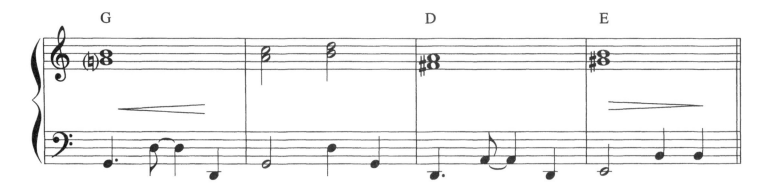

On a dark des- ert high- way,
Her mind is Tif- fa- ny twist- ed.
cool wind in my
She got the Mer- ce- des

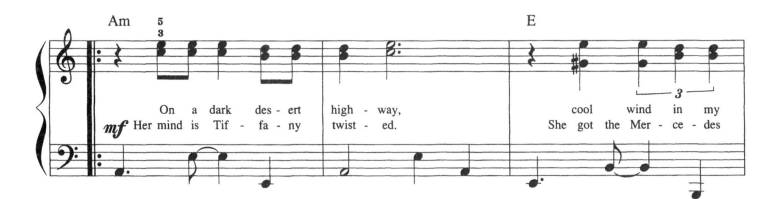

hair,
bends.
warm __ smell of co- li- tas
She got a lot of pret- ty, pret- ty boys

Hotel California - 6 - 2

14

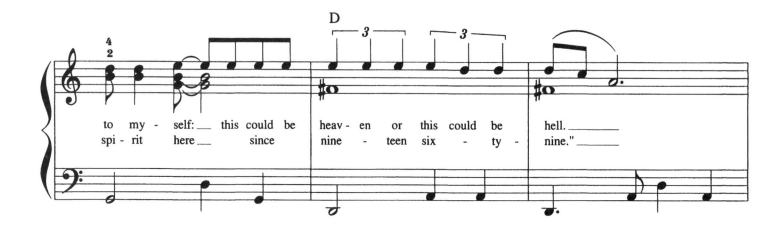

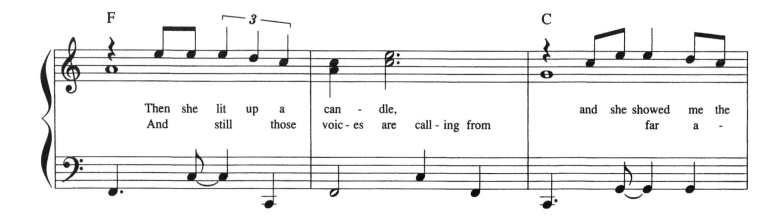

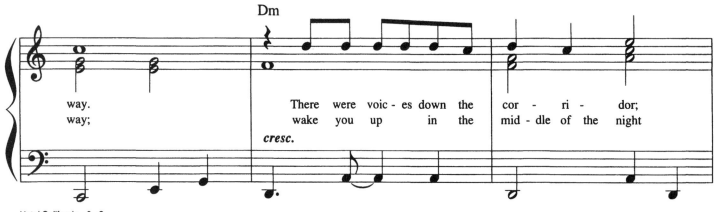

Hotel California - 6 - 3

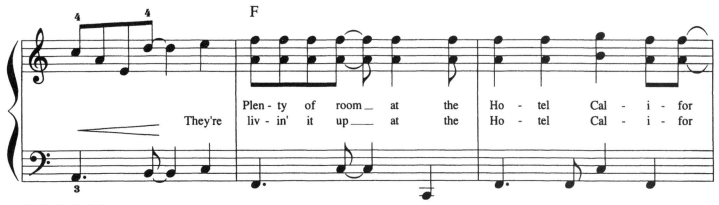

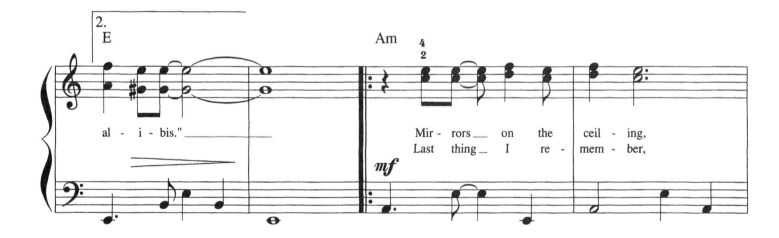

17

# I CAN'T TELL YOU WHY

Words and Music by
DON HENLEY,
GLENN FREY and TIMOTHY B. SCHMIT
*Arranged by DAN COATES*

**Moderately slow**

1. Look at us ba - by, up all night tear - in' our love a - part.
2. *Instrumental*

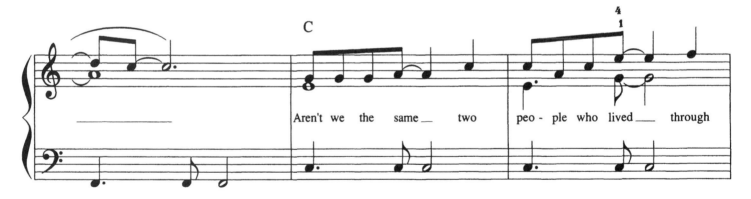

Aren't we the same two peo - ple who lived through

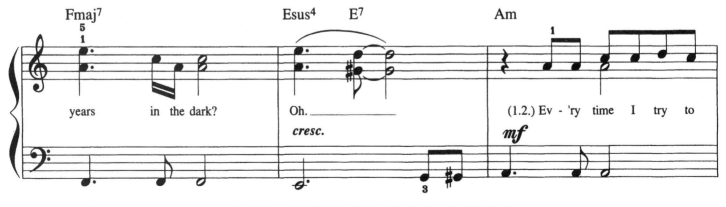

years in the dark? Oh. (1.2.) Ev - 'ry time I try to

I Can't Tell You Why - 4 - 1

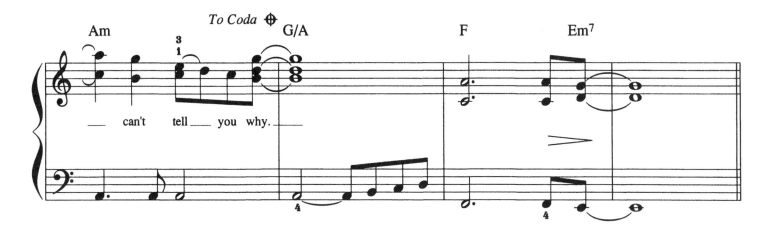

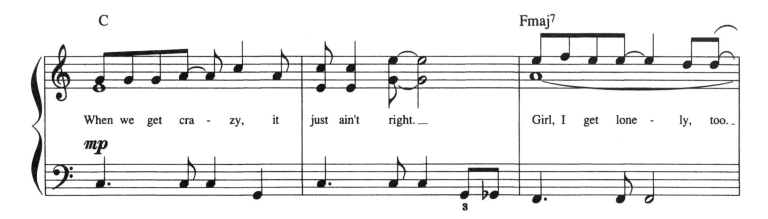

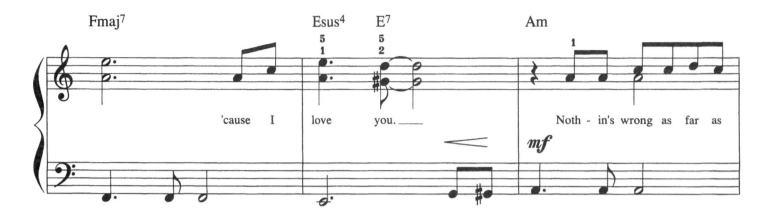

No, no, ba - by, I can't tell you why.

I can't tell you why. I can't tell you why.

# LOVE WILL KEEP US ALIVE

Words and Music by
JIM CAPALDI, PETER VALE
and PAUL CARRACK
*Arranged by DAN COATES*

search - ing _____ for a place to hide. _____
chang - ing _____ right be - fore your eyes. _____
hun - gry, _____ love will keep us a - live. _____

_____ Lost and lone - ly, _____ now you've giv - en me the
_____ Now I've found you, _____ there's no more _____ emp - ti -
_____ (Instrumental solo...)

will to sur - vive. _____ When we're hun - gry, _____
ness _____ in - side. _____ When we're hun - gry, _____
mf

love will keep us a - live. _____
love will keep us a - live. _____
2.) Don't you
mp

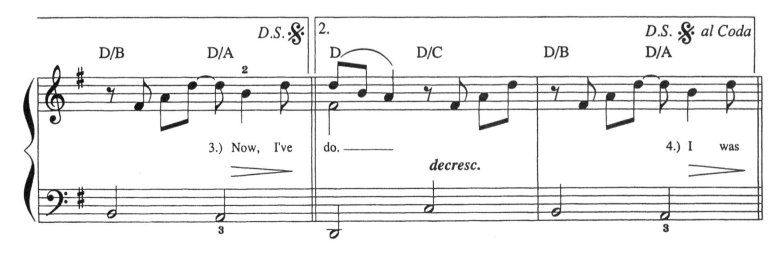

⊕ *Coda*

When we're hun - gry, ———

love will keep us a - live. ———      When we're

hun - gry, ———      love will keep us a - live. ———

*rit.*      *p*

# HEARTACHE TONIGHT

Words and Music by
DON HENLEY, GLENN FREY,
BOB SEGER and JOHN DAVID SOUTHER
*Arranged by DAN COATES*

**Moderate Blues beat**

Heartache Tonight - 5 - 1

G

heart - ache to - night, I know. There's gon - na be a

C7                 *To Coda* ⊕    A

heart - ache to - night, a heart - ache to - night, I know. _____ Lord, I

D        G               Em            G

know.       Some peo - ple like to stay out late. __ Some folks can't hold out that

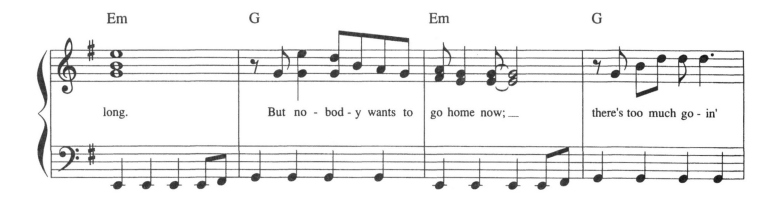

Em        G             Em            G

long.       But no - bod - y wants to go home now; __ there's too much go - in'

28

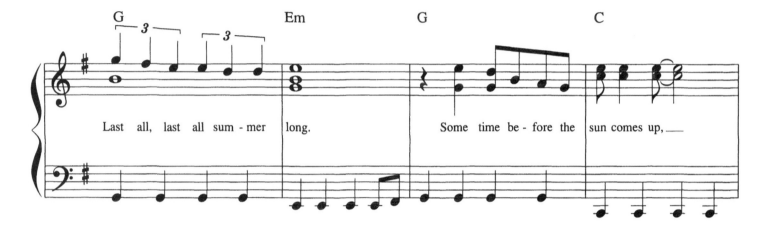

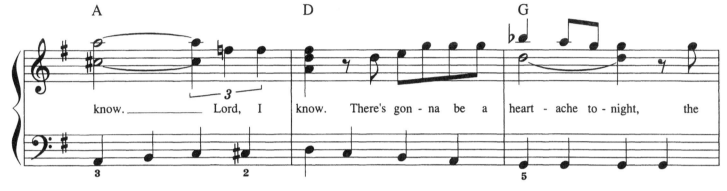

Heartache Tonight - 5 - 4

30

# LYIN' EYES

Words and Music by
DON HENLEY and GLENN FREY
*Arranged by DAN COATES*

**Bright country style** ♩ = 126

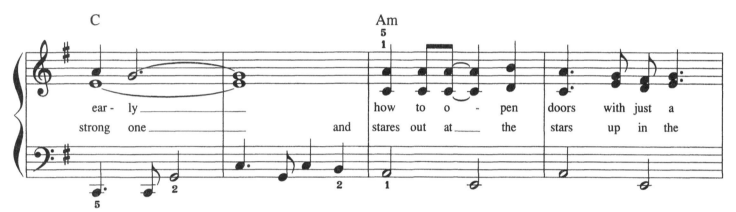

32

Lyin' Eyes - 5 - 2

34

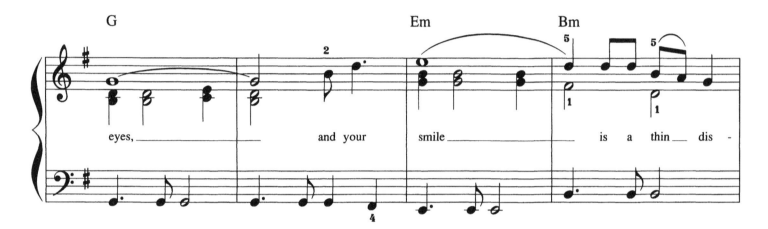

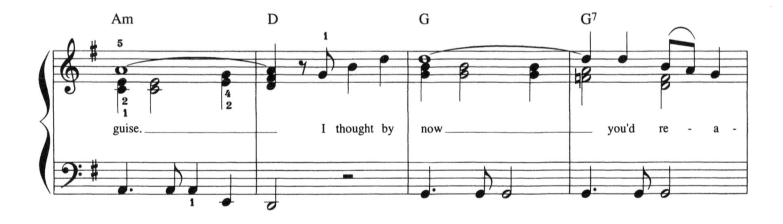

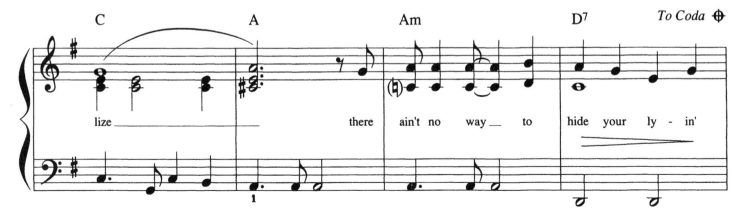

Lyin' Eyes - 5 - 4

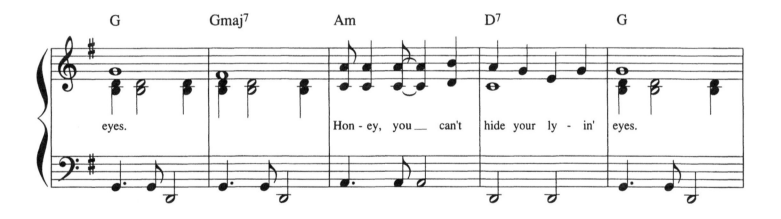

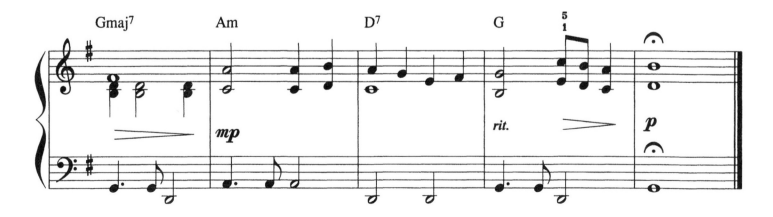

Lyin' Eyes - 5 - 5

# NEW KID IN TOWN

Words and Music by
DON HENLEY,
GLENN FREY and JOHN DAVID SOUTHER
*Arranged by DAN COATES*

Moderately ♩ = 108

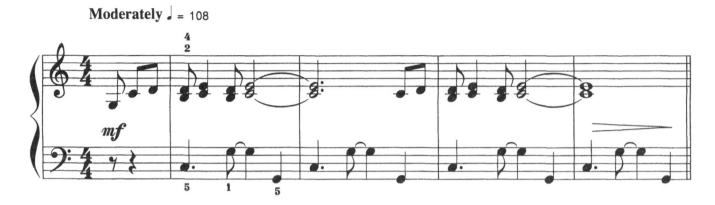

There's talk on the street; it sounds so fa - mil - iar.
You look in her eyes; the mus - ic be - gins to play.

Great ex - pec - ta - tions, ev - 'ry - bod - y's
Hope - less ro - man - tics, here we

watch - ing you.
go a - gain.

Peo - ple you meet,
But af - ter a while

New Kid in Town - 5 - 1

New Kid in Town - 5 - 2

38

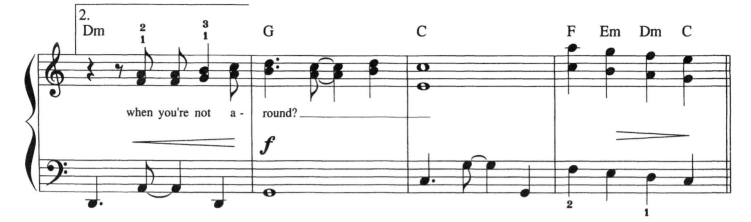

New Kid in Town - 5 - 3

40

# ONE OF THESE NIGHTS

Words and Music by
DON HENLEY and GLENN FREY
*Arranged by DAN COATES*

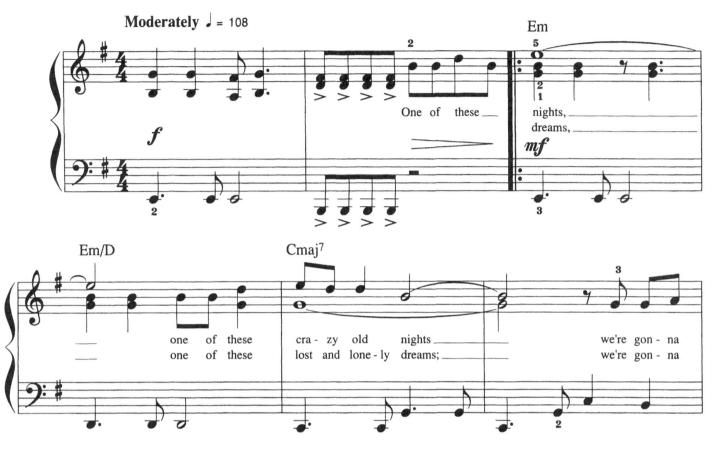

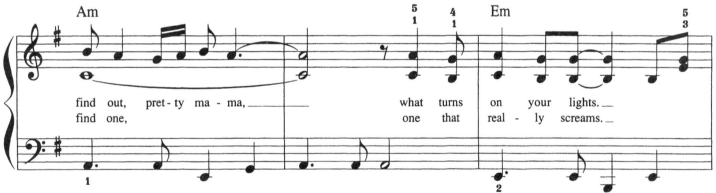

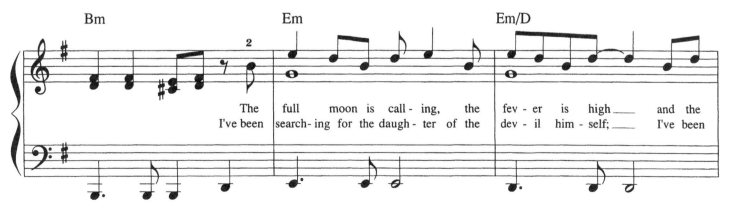

One Of These Nights - 3 - 1

42

One Of These Nights - 3 - 2

One Of These Nights - 3 - 3

# PEACEFUL EASY FEELING

Words and Music by
JACK TEMPCHIN
*Arranged by DAN COATES*

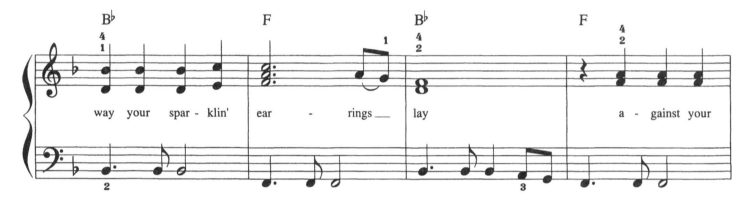

stars all a - round._____ 'Cause I got a peace - ful_____

_ eas - y feel - in',_____ and I know you

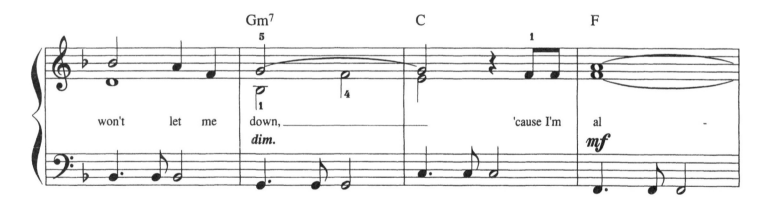

won't let me down,_____ 'cause I'm al -

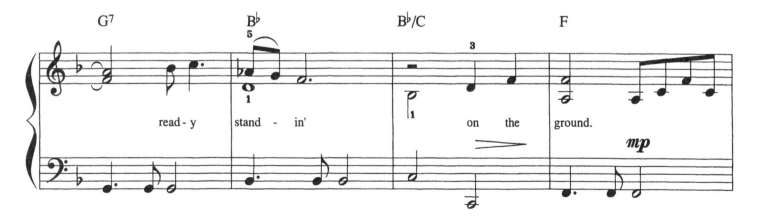

read - y stand - in' on the ground.

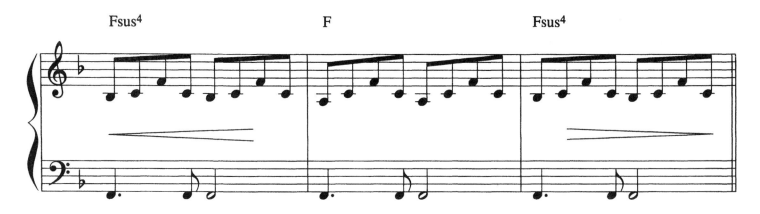

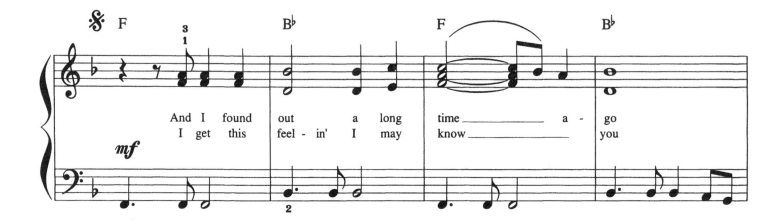

And I found out a long time _____ a - go
I get this feel - in' I may know _____ you

what a wom - an can do to ___ your soul, _____
as a lov - er and ___ a friend, _____

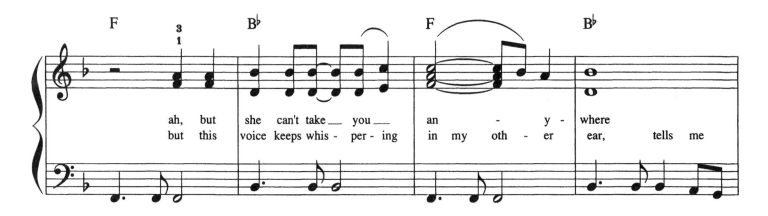

ah, but she can't take ___ you ___ an - y - where
but this voice keeps whis - per - ing in my oth - er ear, tells me

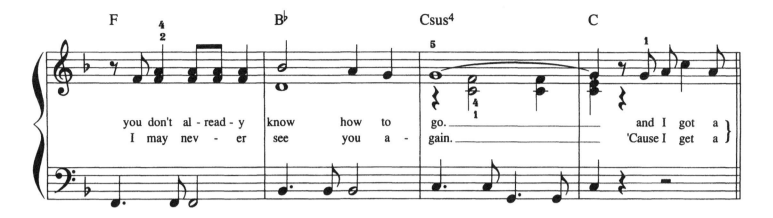

you don't al - read - y know how to go. _____ and I got a
I may nev - er see you a - gain. _____ 'Cause I get a

peace - ful _____ eas - y feel - in', _____

and I know you won't let me down, _____ 'cause I'm

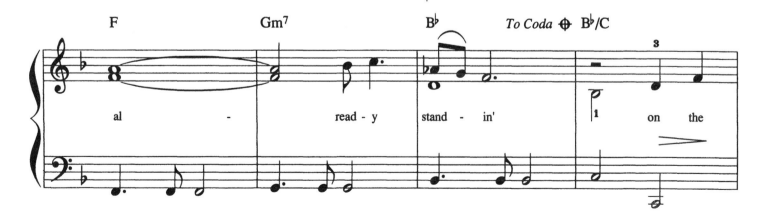

al - read - y stand - in' on the

48

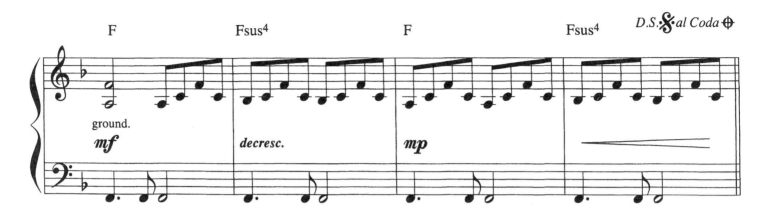

F      Fsus⁴      F      Fsus⁴

ground.
*mf*     *decresc.*     *mp*

*Coda*
⊕   C⁷sus⁴     F     Gm⁷     B♭

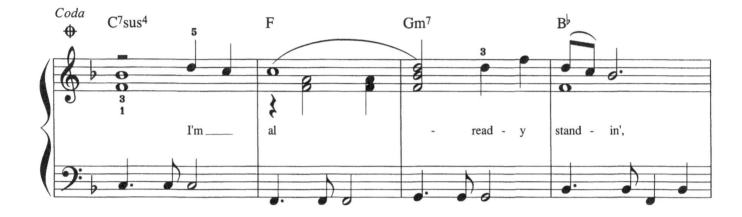

I'm _____ al - read - y stand - in',

C⁷sus⁴     F     Gm⁷     B♭     B♭/C

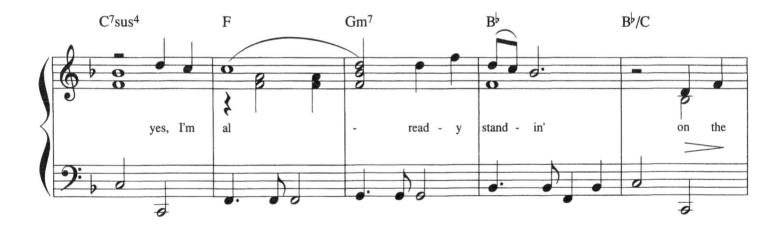

yes, I'm al - read - y stand - in'     on the

F     Gm⁷     B♭     C     F

ground.
*mf*     *rit.*     *mp*

Peaceful Easy Feeling - 5 - 5

# TAKE IT TO THE LIMIT

Words and Music by
DON HENLEY
GLENN FREY and RANDY MEISNER
*Arranged by DAN COATES*

**Moderately slow**

All a-

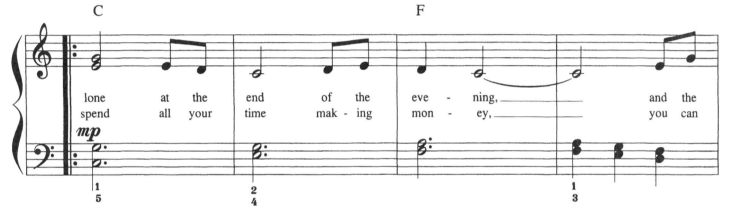

lone at the end of the eve - ning, _____ and the
spend all your time mak - ing mon - ey, _____ you can

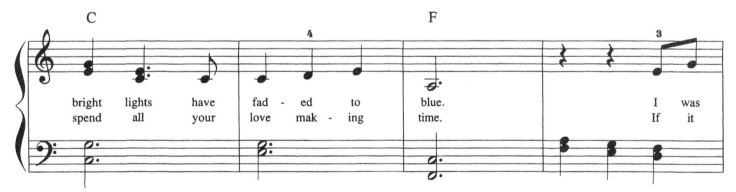

bright lights have fad - ed to blue. I was
spend all your love mak - ing time. If it

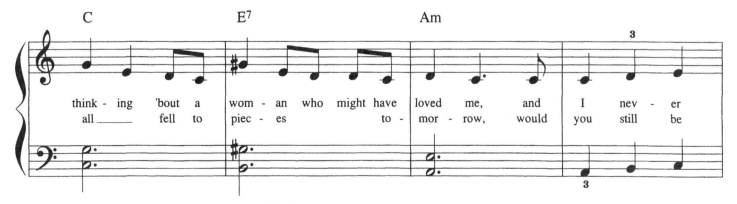

think - ing 'bout a wom - an who might have loved me, and I nev - er
all _____ fell to piec - es to - mor - row, would you still be

50

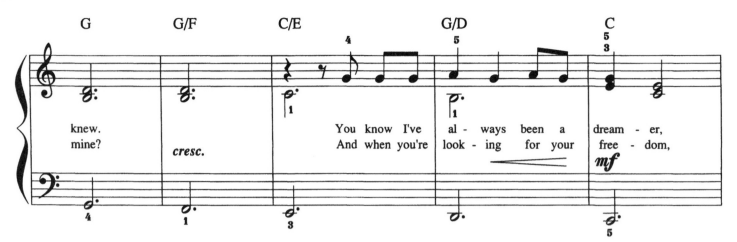

Take It To The Limit - 3 - 2

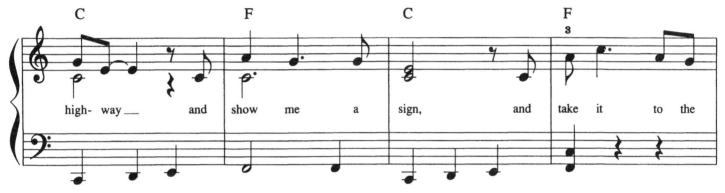

Take It To The Limit - 3 - 3

# TAKE IT EASY

Words and Music by
JACKSON BROWNE and GLENN FREY
*Arranged by DAN COATES*

**Moderate Country feeling** ♩ = 128

1.Well, I'm a - run - nin' down the road try'n' to loos - en my load,___ I've got

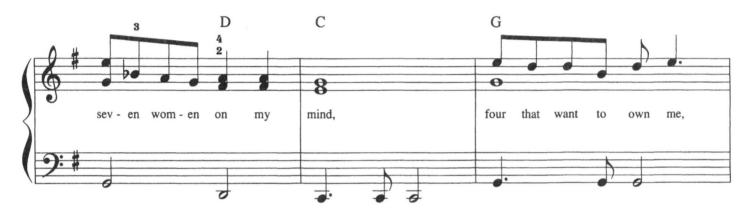

sev - en wom - en on my mind, four that want to own me,

two that wan - na stone me, one says she's a friend___ of mine. Take it

eas - y, take it eas - y. Don't let the

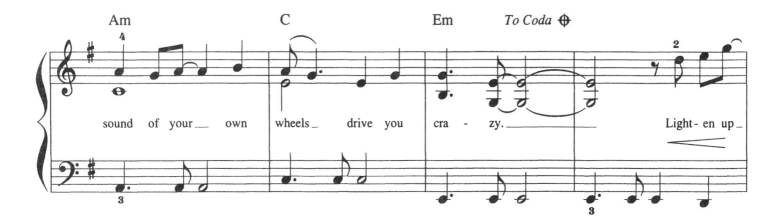

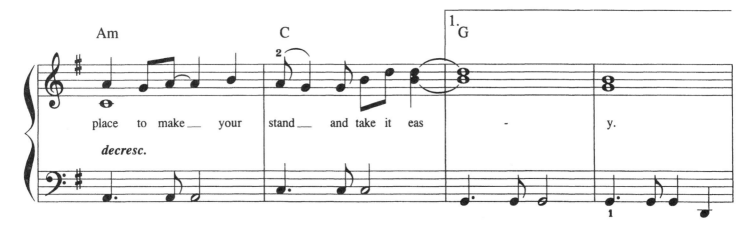

Take It Easy - 4 - 2

54

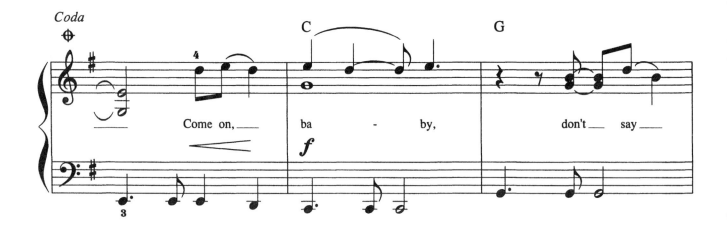

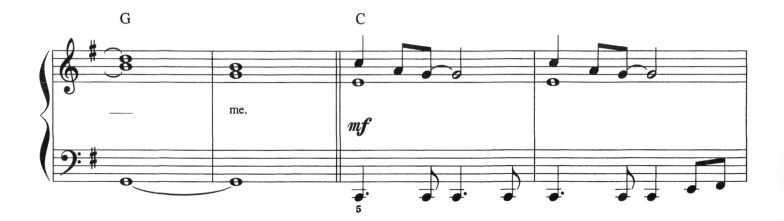

Take It Easy - 4 - 3

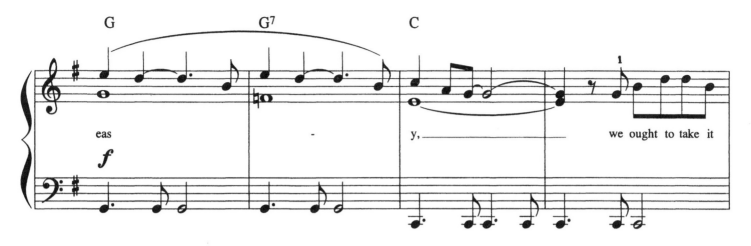

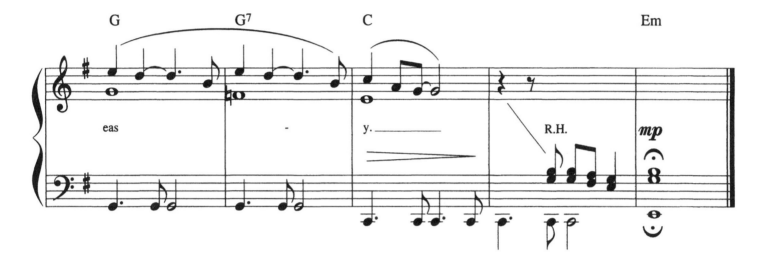

*Verse 2:*
Well, I'm a-standin' on a corner in Winslow, Arizona
And such a fine sight to see,
It's a girl, my Lord, in a flat bed Ford slowin' down to take a look at me.
Come on, baby, don't say maybe,
I gotta know if your sweet love is gonna save me.
We may lose and we may win, though we will never be here again,
So open up, I'm climbin' in, so take it easy.

*Verse 3:*
Well, I'm a-runnin' down the road tryin' to loosen my load,
Got a world of trouble on my mind,
Lookin' for a lover who won't blow my cover, she's so hard to find.
Take it easy, take it easy.
Don't let the sound of your own wheels make you crazy.    *(To Coda:)*